3/07

sgc

DOMESTIC DOGS

GOLDEN RETRIEVERS

by Susan H. Gray

The Child's World

Published in the United States of America by The Child's World®
PO Box 326 • Chanhassen, MN 55317-0326
800-599-READ • www.childsworld.com

PHOTO CREDITS
© Corbis Collection/Alamy: 15
© DLILLC/Corbis: 21
© imagebroker/Alamy: 27
© Juniors Bildarchiv/Alamy: 9, 13
© Mark Raycroft/Minden Pictures: 11, 25
© Paul Barton/Corbis: 17
© Stephanie Sinclair/Corbis: 23
© Stockdisc Classic/Alamy: cover, 1
© tbkmedia.de/Alamy: 19
© Visual&Written SL/Alamy: 29

ACKNOWLEDGMENTS
The Child's World®: Mary Berendes, Publishing Director;
Katherine Stevenson, Editor

The Design Lab: Kathleen Petelinsek, Design and Page Production

LIBRARY OF CONGRESS CATALOGING-IN-PUBLICATION DATA
Gray, Susan Heinrichs.
  Golden retrievers / by Susan H. Gray.
     p. cm. — (Domestic dogs)
Includes bibliographical references and index.
ISBN 1-59296-774-4 (library bound : alk. paper)
1. Golden retriever—Juvenile literature. I. Title. II. Series.
SF429.G63G73 2007
636.752'7—dc22   2006022637

Table of Contents

NAME That DOG!

What big dog has soft, golden hair? ❧ What dog will catch balls and bring them back for hours? ❧ **What dog is friendly and great with kids?** ❧ What dog sometimes finds missing people? ❧ **If you guessed the golden retriever (ree-TREE-vur), you are right!**

5

Golden Water Dogs

In the late 1860s, many people in Great Britain (BRIH-tun) hunted. When they hunted birds, they often took their dogs along. One man, Lord Tweedmouth, had a yellow wavy-coated retriever. It would **retrieve** birds he had shot.

Lord Tweedmouth lived on the Tweed River. Many people there had Tweed water spaniels (SPAN-yulz). These dogs liked to swim. Some people had long-haired Irish setters.

Great Britain is an island in Europe. It includes England, Scotland, and Wales. The map on the left shows where Great Britain is on Earth. The map on the right shows a closer view.

Atlantic Ocean

Scotland

Northern Ireland

Ireland

North Sea

England

Great Britain

Wales

Atlantic Ocean

English Channel

France

Lord Tweedmouth wanted a new kind of dog. He wanted it to be like *all* of these dogs. So he began to **breed** them.

Every time the dogs had puppies, he kept the best ones. He kept the ones with golden coats like his retriever. He kept the ones that swam like water spaniels. He kept the ones with long hair like Irish setters.

When those puppies grew up, *they* had puppies. Again, he kept the best ones. Then they grew up and had puppies. This went on for years.

In time, Lord Tweedmouth had beautiful, long-haired golden dogs. They liked to swim and follow smells. They were the first golden retrievers.

American President Gerald Ford had a golden retriever named Liberty.

This golden retriever's coat looks even more golden when the sun shines on it!

9

Soft, Golden Hair

Golden retrievers are big dogs. They are 21 to 24 inches (53 to 61 centimeters) tall at the shoulder. Most adults weigh 55 to 75 pounds (25 to 34 kilograms). That is about as heavy as a fourth grader.

These dogs are strong and **athletic**. They love to run and swim. They like to retrieve almost anything their owners throw.

Goldens love to run and jump! This one is jumping over boards on a dog course. The course tests how fast a dog can run, turn, and jump.

Golden retriever puppies change colors a little as they grow. Their hair changes to the color of their ears! Older dogs often get gray or white hair on their faces as they age.

Many people think golden retrievers have friendly faces. These dogs have brown eyes and soft ears that hang down. They have black or brown noses. Cold weather can cause their noses to get lighter.

Golden retrievers have two coats of hair. The outer coat is long and thick. It is dark, medium, or light gold. The hair can be straight or wavy. The undercoat has shorter, smoother hair. It keeps the dog warm.

Goldens also have some longer hair, called *feathering*. They have feathering on their necks, chests, legs, and tails.

Golden retrievers have long tails. They hold their tails straight out, or up a little. And they wag them a lot!

A golden retriever's outer coat is called "guard hair."

You can see that parts of this golden's coat are curly. Other parts are straight.

13

One of the Top Dogs

Golden retrievers make great pets. They are one of America's three most **popular** dogs. They love to please their owners. They love to be with people. They are friendly, smart, gentle, and easy to train.

Goldens can learn all kinds of tricks! They can learn to sit and stay, roll over, and play dead. But they can also learn to get the newspaper. They can learn to open the refrigerator. They can learn to retrieve just about anything.

This girl is teaching her golden to sit up. He will get a treat for doing a good job.

15

Golden retrievers can be handy to have around! And they work on learning tricks until they are worn out. All of this makes training fun.

Golden retrievers are great family dogs. They are gentle with children. They love to go camping and hiking. They are happiest when they are part of the family.

Their friendly ways can be too much for some people. These dogs need lots of attention. People who are always at work should not have goldens. Very small homes are not good for them, either. These dogs like to run around and exercise. They need to play in the yard or go to a park.

Golden retrievers are good swimmers. Their coats shed water easily.

Goldens are very loyal dogs. They like to be near their owners, even when it is time to rest or sleep.

Little Golden Babies

Golden retriever mothers often have about eight puppies in a **litter**. Some have smaller litters, and some have larger ones. Each newborn puppy weighs less than a pound (half a kilogram).

Newborn goldens are weak and helpless. They cannot hear. Their eyes are closed. Their legs are too weak for walking.

This golden mother has a big litter! How many puppies can you see?

Golden retriever pups have very short, soft coats. As they grow, their hair gets longer. In time, they grow their long, feathered coats.

The puppies' first few weeks are very important. This is when they get used to other dogs. They also get used to people. At first, they just want to be with their family. They feel safe near their mother, brothers, and sisters.

In the first month, the puppies can be held. But they should be held gently—and not for very long. In their second month, the puppies get braver. They begin to run around. They do not go far, though. They still feel safer with their family. But soon they are ready to go to their new families.

Young goldens love to carry things around. They proudly carry sticks or toys—or people's shoes!

These golden puppies are about five weeks old. They all want to carry the same stick.

Golden Retrievers on the Job

Many people keep golden retrievers as pets. But some goldens have other jobs. Some work for the police. Some are "Search and **Rescue**" dogs. These dogs look for people who are lost or in danger. Sometimes buildings fall down because of storms or other **disasters**. The dogs help find people who are buried. They can find them with their sense of smell. Their work saves many lives.

This golden is helping search for people after an explosion in Iraq.

When a service dog is working, people should leave it alone. They should not pet it or bother it. The dog needs to pay attention to what it is doing.

Other golden retrievers work as **service** dogs. They work with people who need special help. **Guide** dogs help people who cannot see. They go everywhere with their owners. They help them cross streets and go down stairs.

Other service dogs help people who have trouble doing other things. These dogs sometimes pull wheelchairs. They turn lights on and off. They even take off their owner's socks.

Service dogs often wear something that says they are working. Then people know they are service dogs. Service dogs can go in offices, stores, and banks.

Many kinds of dogs work as service dogs. But two kinds seem to be the best. They are golden retrievers and Labrador retrievers.

24

Both service and guide dogs wear special packs on their backs. The packs carry things the owner needs, such as medicine or keys.

25

Caring for a Golden Retriever

Golden retrievers are big dogs that need plenty of exercise. Running around the house is not enough. They need to go outside and play. Goldens that are stuck inside can get lazy. They can also gain weight.

A golden retriever's long, soft coat should be brushed often. Otherwise, it can get tangled or dirty. Some goldens have skin problems. Some are **allergic** to things like dust, flowers, or fleas. Allergies might make their hair fall out or their skin turn red. They might scratch or lick a lot.

There are lots of different brushes you can buy for dogs. This brush is good for a golden's thick coat.

27

Some golden retrievers have heart problems. Others have problems with their eyes. Some golden retrievers have hip problems. So do many other large dogs. Their leg bones slide out of place. This can happen even in puppies. It can cause pain or problems walking. Animal doctors can help with these and other problems.

Most golden retrievers live long, happy lives. Most of them live to be 10 or 12 years old. Some live to be 15 or 16. And they are much-loved members of their families!

There are lots of golden retrievers on TV. Dogs named Comet and Speedy have been in weekly shows. Dogs named Alex and Duke have been in commercials.

Goldens are happiest when they can run, play, and be with their owners. This golden looks very happy!

29

Glossary

allergic (uh-LUR-jik) If you are allergic to something, your body reacts badly to it. Some golden retrievers have allergies.

athletic (ath-LEH-tik) Someone who is athletic is very good at sports. Golden retrievers are athletic.

breed (BREED) To breed animals is to choose which parents will have babies. Lord Tweedmouth bred the best dogs he could find.

disasters (dih-ZASS-turs) Disasters are events that cause terrible loss or suffering. Some golden retrievers look for lost people after disasters.

guide (GIDE) To guide people is to lead them or help them find their way. Guide dogs help people who cannot see.

litter (LIH-tur) A litter is a group of babies born to one animal. Golden retrievers often have litters of about eight puppies.

popular (PAH-pyuh-lur) When something is popular, it is liked by lots of people. Golden retrievers are very popular.

rescue (RESS-kyoo) To rescue something is to save it from danger. Some golden retrievers work as "Search and Rescue" dogs.

retrieve (rih-TREEV) To retrieve something is to find it and bring it back. Golden retrievers learn to retrieve easily.

service (SUR-vuss) Service is work that helps someone. Golden retrievers often make great service dogs.

To Find Out More

Books to Read

Feldman, Heather L. *The Story of the Golden Retriever.* New York: PowerKids Press, 2000.

Hubbard, Coleen. *One Golden Year: A Story of a Golden Retriever.* New York: Scholastic, 1998.

Huxley, Joanne P. *Guide to Owning a Golden Retriever.* Philadelphia, PA: Chelsea House, 1995.

Patent, Dorothy Hinshaw. *Right Dog for the Job: Ira's Path from Service Dog to Guide Dog.* New York: Walker & Company, 2004.

Stone, Lynn M. *Golden Retrievers.* Vero Beach, FL: Rourke Publishing, 2003.

Places to Contact

American Kennel Club (AKC) Headquarters
260 Madison Ave, New York, NY 10016
Telephone: 212-696-8200

On the Web

Visit our Web site for lots of links about golden retrievers:

http://www.childsworld.com/links

Note to Parents, Teachers, and Librarians: We routinely check our Web links to make sure they're safe, active sites—so encourage your readers to check them out!

Index

About the Author

Susan H. Gray has a Master's degree in zoology. She has written more than 70 science and reference books for children. She loves to garden and play the piano. Susan lives in Cabot, Arkansas, with her husband Michael and many pets.